POETRY FIRST

1914 and Oth

RUPERT BI

RUPERT BROOKE (1887–1915)

1914 and Other Poems first published 1915

RUPERT BROOKE

1914 and Other Poems

with a Note on the Text by
Michael Schmidt

PENGUIN BOOKS

PENGUIN BOOKS

Published by the Penguin Group
Penguin Books Ltd, 27 Wrights Lane, London w8 5tz, England
Penguin Putnam Inc., 375 Hudson Street, New York, New York 10014, USA
Penguin Books Australia Ltd, Ringwood, Victoria, Australia
Penguin Books Canada Ltd, 10 Alcorn Avenue, Toronto, Ontario, Canada m4v 3b2
Penguin Books (NZ) Ltd, Private Bag 102902, NSMC, Auckland, New Zealand

Penguin Books Ltd, Registered Offices: Harmondsworth, Middlesex, England

Published in Penguin Books 1999
1 3 5 7 9 10 8 6 4 2

The front cover shows *The Cinder Path*, 1912, by Spencer Gore
© Tate Gallery, London

Set in 11/14 pt PostScript Monotype Baskerville
Typeset by Rowland Phototypesetting Ltd, Bury St Edmunds, Suffolk
Printed in England by Clays Ltd, St Ives plc

RUPERT BROOKE

Born at Rugby, August 3, 1887
Fellow of King's, 1913
Sub-Lieutenant, R.N.V.R., September 1914
Antwerp Expedition, October 1914
Sailed with British Mediterranean
   Expeditionary Force, February 28, 1915
Died in the Ægean, April 23, 1915

These poems have appeared in *New Numbers*, the old *Poetry Review*, *Poetry and Drama*, *Rhythm*, *The Blue Review*, *The New Statesman*, *The Pall Mall Magazine*, and *Basileon*. Acknowledgements are due to the Editors who have allowed them to be reprinted.

The Author had thought of publishing a volume of poems this spring, but he did not prepare the present book for publication.

May 1915   E. M.

CONTENTS

1914

I. Peace   3
II. Safety   4
III. The Dead   5
IV. The Dead   6
V. The Soldier   7
The Treasure   8

THE SOUTH SEAS

Tiare Tahiti   11
Retrospect   14
The Great Lover   16
Heaven   19
Doubts   21
There's Wisdom in Women   22
He wonders whether to praise or
    to blame her   23
A Memory   24
One Day   25
Waikiki   26
Hauntings   27
Sonnet (SUGGESTED BY SOME
    OF THE PROCEEDINGS
    OF THE SOCIETY FOR
    PSYCHICAL RESEARCH)   28
Clouds   29
Mutability   30

OTHER POEMS

The Busy Heart	33
Love	34
Unfortunate	35
The Chilterns	36
Home	38
The Night Journey	39
Song	41
Beauty and Beauty	42
The Way that Lovers use	43
Mary and Gabriel	44
The Funeral of Youth	46

GRANTCHESTER

The Old Vicarage, Grantchester	49

1914

I. Peace

Now, God be thanked Who has matched us with His hour,
　　And caught our youth, and wakened us from sleeping,
With hand made sure, clear eye, and sharpened power,
　　To turn, as swimmers into cleanness leaping,
Glad from a world grown old and cold and weary,
　　Leave the sick hearts that honour could not move,
And half-men, and their dirty songs and dreary,
　　And all the little emptiness of love!

Oh! we, who have known shame, we have found release there,
　　Where there's no ill, no grief, but sleep has mending,
　　　　Naught broken save this body, lost but breath;
Nothing to shake the laughing heart's long peace there
　　But only agony, and that has ending;
　　　　And the worst friend and enemy is but Death.

II. Safety

Dear! of all happy in the hour, most blest
   He who has found our hid security,
Assured in the dark tides of the world that rest,
   And heard our word, 'Who is so safe as we?'
We have found safety with all things undying,
   The winds, and morning, tears of men and mirth,
The deep night, and birds singing, and clouds flying,
   And sleep, and freedom, and the autumnal earth.
We have built a house that is not for Time's throwing.
   We have gained a peace unshaken by pain for ever.
War knows no power. Safe shall be my going,
   Secretly armed against all death's endeavour;
Safe though all safety's lost; safe where men fall;
And if these poor limbs die, safest of all.

III. *The Dead*

Blow out, you bugles, over the rich Dead!
   There's none of these so lonely and poor of old,
   But, dying, has made us rarer gifts than gold.
These laid the world away; poured out the red
Sweet wine of youth; gave up the years to be
   Of work and joy, and that unhoped serene,
   That men call age; and those who would have been,
Their sons, they gave, their immortality.

Blow, bugles, blow! They brought us, for our dearth,
   Holiness, lacked so long, and Love, and Pain.
Honour has come back, as a king, to earth,
   And paid his subjects with a royal wage;
And Nobleness walks in our ways again;
   And we have come into our heritage.

IV. The Dead

These hearts were woven of human joys and cares,
　　Washed marvellously with sorrow, swift to mirth.
The years had given them kindness. Dawn was theirs,
　　And sunset, and the colours of the earth.
These had seen movement, and heard music; known
　　Slumber and waking; loved; gone proudly friended;
Felt the quick stir of wonder; sat alone;
　　Touched flowers and furs and cheeks. All this is ended.

There are waters blown by changing winds to laughter
And lit by the rich skies, all day. And after,
　　Frost, with a gesture, stays the waves that dance
And wandering loveliness. He leaves a white
　　Unbroken glory, a gathered radiance,
A width, a shining peace, under the night.

V. The Soldier

If I should die, think only this of me:
   That there's some corner of a foreign field
That is for ever England. There shall be
   In that rich earth a richer dust concealed;
A dust whom England bore, shaped, made aware,
   Gave, once, her flowers to love, her ways to roam,
A body of England's, breathing English air,
   Washed by the rivers, blest by suns of home.

And think, this heart, all evil shed away,
   A pulse in the eternal mind, no less
     Gives somewhere back the thoughts by England
       given;
Her sights and sounds; dreams happy as her day;
   And laughter, learnt of friends; and gentleness,
     In hearts at peace, under an English heaven.

The Treasure

When colour goes home into the eyes,
   And lights that shine are shut again
With dancing girls and sweet birds' cries
   Behind the gateways of the brain;
And that no-place which gave them birth, shall close
The rainbow and the rose:

Still may Time hold some golden space
   Where I'll unpack that scented store
Of song and flower and sky and face,
   And count, and touch, and turn them o'er,
Musing upon them; as a mother, who
Has watched her children all the rich day through,
Sits, quiet-handed, in the fading light,
When children sleep, ere night.

THE SOUTH SEAS

Tiare Tahiti

Mamua, when our laughter ends,
And hearts and bodies, brown as white,
Are dust about the doors of friends,
Or scent ablowing down the night,
Then, oh! then, the wise agree,
Comes our immortality.
Mamua, there waits a land
Hard for us to understand.
Out of time, beyond the sun,
All are one in Paradise,
You and Pupure are one,
And Taü, and the ungainly wise.
There the Eternals are, and there
The Good, the Lovely, and the True,
And Types, whose earthly copies were
The foolish broken things we knew;
There is the Face, whose ghosts we are;
The real, the never-setting Star;
And the Flower, of which we love
Faint and fading shadows here;
Never a tear, but only Grief;
Dance, but not the limbs that move;
Songs in Song shall disappear;
Instead of lovers, Love shall be;
For hearts, Immutability;
And there, on the Ideal Reef,
Thunders the Everlasting Sea!
    And my laughter, and my pain,
Shall home to the Eternal Brain.
And all lovely things, they say,
Meet in Loveliness again;

Miri's laugh, Teïpo's feet,
And the hands of Matua,
Stars and sunlight there shall meet,
Coral's hues and rainbows there,
And Teüra's braided hair;
And with the starred *tiare's* white,
And white birds in the dark ravine,
And *flamboyants* ablaze at night,
And jewels, and evening's after-green,
And dawns of pearl and gold and red,
Mamua, your lovelier head!
And there'll no more be one who dreams
Under the ferns, of crumbling stuff,
Eyes of illusion, mouth that seems,
All time-entangled human love.
And you'll no longer swing and sway
Divinely down the scented shade,
Where feet to Ambulation fade,
And moons are lost in endless Day.
How shall we wind these wreaths of ours,
Where there are neither heads nor flowers?
Oh, Heaven's Heaven! – but we'll be missing
The palms, and sunlight, and the south;
And there's an end, I think, of kissing,
When our mouths are one with Mouth . . .

   Taü here, Mamua,
Crown the hair, and come away!
Hear the calling of the moon,
And the whispering scents that stray
About the idle warm lagoon.
Hasten, hand in human hand,
Down the dark, the flowered way,
Along the whiteness of the sand,
And in the water's soft caress,
Wash the mind of foolishness,

Mamua, until the day.
Spend the glittering moonlight there
Pursuing down the soundless deep
Limbs that gleam and shadowy hair,
Or floating lazy, half-asleep.
Dive and double and follow after,
Snare in flowers, and kiss, and call,
With lips that fade, and human laughter
And faces individual,
Well this side of Paradise! . . .
There's little comfort in the wise.

PAPEETE, *February* 1914

Retrospect

In your arms was still delight,
Quiet as a street at night;
And thoughts of you, I do remember,
Were green leaves in a darkened chamber,
Were dark clouds in a moonless sky.
Love, in you, went passing by,
Penetrative, remote, and rare,
Like a bird in the wide air,
And, as the bird, it left no trace
In the heaven of your face.
In your stupidity I found
The sweet hush after a sweet sound.
All about you was the light
That dims the greying end of night;
Desire was the unrisen sun,
Joy the day not yet begun,
With tree whispering to tree,
Without wind, quietly.
Wisdom slept within your hair,
And Long-Suffering was there,
And, in the flowing of your dress,
Undiscerning Tenderness.
And when you thought, it seemed to me,
Infinitely, and like a sea,
About the slight world you had known
Your vast unconsciousness was thrown . . .
    O haven without wave or tide!
Silence, in which all songs have died!
Holy book, where hearts are still!
And home at length under the hill!
O mother quiet, breasts of peace,
Where love itself would faint and cease!

O infinite deep I never knew,
I would come back, come back to you,
Find you, as a pool unstirred,
Kneel down by you, and never a word,
Lay my head, and nothing said,
In your hands, ungarlanded;
And a long watch you would keep;
And I should sleep, and I should sleep!

MATAIEA, *January* 1914

The Great Lover

I have been so great a lover: filled my days
So proudly with the splendour of Love's praise,
The pain, the calm, and the astonishment,
Desire illimitable, and still content,
And all dear names men use, to cheat despair,
For the perplexed and viewless streams that bear
Our hearts at random down the dark of life.
Now, ere the unthinking silence on that strife
Steals down, I would cheat drowsy Death so far,
My night shall be remembered for a star
That outshone all the suns of all men's days.
Shall I not crown them with immortal praise
Whom I have loved, who have given me, dared with me
High secrets, and in darkness knelt to see
The inenarrable godhead of delight?
Love is a flame – we have beaconed the world's night.
A city – and we have built it, these and I.
An emperor – we have taught the world to die.
So, for their sakes I loved, ere I go hence,
And the high cause of Love's magnificence,
And to keep loyalties young, I'll write those names
Golden for ever, eagles, crying flames,
And set them as a banner, that men may know,
To dare the generations, burn, and blow
Out on the wind of Time, shining and streaming . . .
These I have loved:

                White plates and cups, clean-gleaming,
Ringed with blue lines; and feathery, faery dust;
Wet roofs, beneath the lamp-light; the strong crust
Of friendly bread; and many-tasting food;
Rainbows; and the blue bitter smoke of wood;

And radiant raindrops couching in cool flowers;
And flowers themselves, that sway through sunny hours,
Dreaming of moths that drink them under the moon;
Then, the cool kindliness of sheets, that soon
Smooth away trouble; and the rough male kiss
Of blankets; grainy wood; live hair that is
Shining and free; blue-massing clouds; the keen
Unpassioned beauty of a great machine;
The benison of hot water; furs to touch;
The good smell of old clothes; and other such –
The comfortable smell of friendly fingers,
Hair's fragrance, and the musty reek that lingers
About dead leaves and last year's ferns . . .

Dear names,

And thousand other throng to me! Royal flames;
Sweet water's dimpling laugh from tap or spring;
Holes in the ground; and voices that do sing;
Voices in laughter, too; and body's pain,
Soon turned to peace; and the deep-panting train;
Firm sands; the little dulling edge of foam
That browns and dwindles as the wave goes home;
And washen stones, gay for an hour; the cold
Graveness of iron; moist black earthen mould;
Sleep; and high places; footprints in the dew;
And oaks; and brown horse-chestnuts, glossy-new;
And new-peeled sticks; and shining pools on grass –
All these have been my loves. And these shall pass,
Whatever passes not, in the great hour,
Nor all my passion, all my prayers, have power
To hold them with me through the gate of Death.
They'll play deserter, turn with the traitor breath,
Break the high bond we made, and sell Love's trust
And sacramented covenant to the dust.
——Oh, never a doubt but, somewhere, I shall wake,
And give what's left of love again, and make

New friends, now strangers . . .

                      But the best I've known,
Stays here, and changes, breaks, grows old, is blown
About the winds of the world, and fades from brains
Of living men, and dies.

                    Nothing remains.

O dear my loves, O faithless, once again
This one last gift I give: that after men
Shall know, and later lovers, far-removed,
Praise you, 'All these were lovely'; say, 'He loved.'

                              MATAIEA, 1914

Heaven

Fish (fly-replete, in depth of June,
Dawdling away their wat'ry noon)
Ponder deep wisdom, dark or clear,
Each secret fishy hope or fear.
Fish say, they have their Stream and Pond;
But is there anything Beyond?
This life cannot be All, they swear,
For how unpleasant, if it were!
One may not doubt that, somehow, Good
Shall come of Water and of Mud;
And, sure, the reverent eye must see
A Purpose in Liquidity.
We darkly know, by Faith we cry,
The future is not Wholly Dry.
Mud unto mud! – Death eddies near –
Not here the appointed End, not here!
But somewhere, beyond Space and Time,
Is wetter water, slimier slime!
And there (they trust) there swimmeth One
Who swam ere rivers were begun,
Immense, of fishy form and mind,
Squamous, omnipotent, and kind;
And under that Almighty Fin,
The littlest fish may enter in.
Oh! never fly conceals a hook,
Fish say, in the Eternal Brook,
But more than mundane weeds are there,
And mud, celestially fair;

Fat caterpillars drift around,
And Paradisal grubs are found;
Unfading moths, immortal flies,
And the worm that never dies.
And in that Heaven of all their wish,
There shall be no more land, say fish.

Doubts

When she sleeps, her soul, I know,
Goes a wanderer on the air,
Wings where I may never go,
Leaves her lying, still and fair,
Waiting, empty, laid aside,
Like a dress upon a chair . . .
This I know, and yet I know
Doubts that will not be denied.

For if the soul be not in place,
What has laid trouble in her face?
And, sits there nothing ware and wise
Behind the curtains of her eyes,
What is it, in the self's eclipse,
Shadows, soft and passingly,
About the corners of her lips,
The smile that is essential she?

And if the spirit be not there,
Why is fragrance in the hair?

There's Wisdom in Women

'Oh love is fair, and love is rare;' my dear one she said,
'But love goes lightly over.' I bowed her foolish head,
And kissed her hair and laughed at her. Such a child was she;
So new to love, so true to love, and she spoke so bitterly.

But there's wisdom in women, of more than they have
      known,
And thoughts go blowing through them, are wiser than their
      own,
Or how should my dear one, being ignorant and young,
Have cried on love so bitterly, with so true a tongue?

He wonders whether to praise
or to blame her

I have peace to weigh your worth, now all is over,
    But if to praise or blame you, cannot say.
For, who decries the loved, decries the lover;
    Yet what man lauds the thing he's thrown away?

Be you, in truth, this dull, slight, cloudy naught,
    The more fool I, so great a fool to adore;
But if you're that high goddess once I thought,
    The more your godhead is, I lose the more.

Dear fool, pity the fool who thought you clever!
    Dear wisdom, do not mock the fool that missed you!
Most fair – the blind has lost your face for ever!
    Most foul – how could I see you while I kissed you?

So . . . the poor love of fools and blind I've proved you,
For, foul or lovely, 'twas a fool that loved you.

A Memory
(FROM A SONNET-SEQUENCE)

Somewhile before the dawn I rose, and stept
   Softly along the dim way to your room,
   And found you sleeping in the quiet gloom,
And holiness about you as you slept.
I knelt there; till your waking fingers crept
   About my head, and held it. I had rest
   Unhoped this side of Heaven, beneath your breast.
I knelt a long time, still; nor even wept.

It was great wrong you did me; and for gain
Of that poor moment's kindliness, and ease,
And sleepy mother-comfort!
                Child, you know
How easily love leaps out to dreams like these,
Who has seen them true. And love that's wakened so
Takes all too long to lay asleep again.

                    WAIKIKI, *October* 1913

One Day

Today I have been happy. All the day
   I held the memory of you, and wove
Its laughter with the dancing light o' the spray,
   And sowed the sky with tiny clouds of love,
And sent you following the white waves of sea,
   And crowned your head with fancies, nothing worth,
Stray buds from that old dust of misery,
   Being glad with a new foolish quiet mirth.

So lightly I played with those dark memories,
Just as a child, beneath the summer skies,
   Plays hour by hour with a strange shining stone,
For which (he knows not) towns were fire of old,
   And love has been betrayed, and murder done,
And great kings turned to a little bitter mould.

THE PACIFIC, *October* 1913

Waikiki

Warm perfumes like a breath from vine and tree
    Drift down the darkness. Plangent, hidden from eyes,
    Somewhere an *eukaleli* thrills and cries
And stabs with pain the night's brown savagery.
And dark scents whisper; and dim waves creep to me,
    Gleam like a woman's hair, stretch out, and rise;
    And new stars burn into the ancient skies,
Over the murmurous soft Hawaian sea.

And I recall, lose, grasp, forget again,
    And still remember, a tale I have heard, or known
An empty tale, of idleness and pain,
    Of two that loved – or did not love – and one
Whose perplexed heart did evil, foolishly,
A long while since, and by some other sea.

WAIKIKI, 1913

Hauntings

In the grey tumult of these after years
   Oft silence falls; the incessant wranglers part;
And less-than-echoes of remembered tears
   Hush all the loud confusion of the heart;
And a shade, through the toss'd ranks of mirth and crying
   Hungers, and pains, and each dull passionate mood –
Quite lost, and all but all forgot, undying
   Comes back the ecstasy of your quietude.

So a poor ghost, beside his misty streams,
Is haunted by strange doubts, evasive dreams,
   Hints of a pre-Lethean life, of men,
Stars, rocks, and flesh, things unintelligible,
   And light on waving grass, he knows not when,
And feet that ran, but where, he cannot tell.

THE PACIFIC, 1914

Sonnet

(SUGGESTED BY SOME OF THE PROCEEDINGS OF THE SOCIETY FOR PSYCHICAL RESEARCH)

Not with vain tears, when we're beyond the sun,
 We'll beat on the substantial doors, nor tread
 Those dusty high-roads of the aimless dead
Plaintive for Earth; but rather turn and run
Down some close-covered by-way of the air,
 Some low sweet alley between wind and wind,
 Stoop under faint gleams, thread the shadows, find
Some whispering ghost-forgotten nook, and there

Spend in pure converse our eternal day;
 Think each in each, immediately wise;
Learn all we lacked before; hear, know, and say
 What this tumultuous body now denies;
And feel, who have laid our groping hands away;
 And see, no longer blinded by our eyes.

Clouds

Down the blue night the unending columns press
In noiseless tumult, break and wave and flow,
Now tread the far South, or lift rounds of snow
Up to the white moon's hidden loveliness.
Some pause in their grave wandering comradeless,
And turn with profound gesture vague and slow,
As who would pray good for the world, but know
Their benediction empty as they bless.

They say that the Dead die not, but remain
Near to the rich heirs of their grief and mirth.
I think they ride the calm mid-heaven, as these,
In wise majestic melancholy train,
And watch the moon, and the still-raging seas,
And men, coming and going on the earth.

THE PACIFIC, *October* 1913

Mutability

They say there's a high windless world and strange,
    Out of the wash of days and temporal tide,
    Where Faith and Good, Wisdom and Truth abide,
Æterna corpora, subject to no change.
There the sure suns of these pale shadows move;
    There stand the immortal ensigns of our war;
    Our melting flesh fixed Beauty there, a star,
And perishing hearts, imperishable Love . . .

Dear, we know only that we sigh, kiss, smile;
    Each kiss lasts but the kissing; and grief goes over;
    Love has no habitation but the heart.
Poor straws! on the dark flood we catch awhile,
    Cling, and are borne into the night apart.
    The laugh dies with the lips, 'Love' with the lover.

SOUTH KENSINGTON—MAKAWELI, 1913

OTHER POEMS

The Busy Heart

Now that we've done our best and worst, and parted,
   I would fill my mind with thoughts that will not rend.
(O heart, I do not dare go empty-hearted)
   I'll think of Love in books, Love without end;
Women with child, content; and old men sleeping;
   And wet strong ploughlands, scarred for certain grain;
And babes that weep, and so forget their weeping;
   And the young heavens, forgetful after rain;
And evening hush, broken by homing wings;
   And Song's nobility, and Wisdom holy,
That live, we dead. I would think of a thousand things,
   Lovely and durable, and taste them slowly,
One after one, like tasting a sweet food.
I have need to busy my heart with quietude.

Love

Love is a breach in the walls, a broken gate,
    Where that comes in that shall not go again;
Love sells the proud heart's citadel to Fate.
    They have known shame, who love unloved. Even then
When two mouths, thirsty each for each, find slaking,
    And agony's forgot, and hushed the crying
Of credulous hearts, in heaven – such are but taking
    Their own poor dreams within their arms, and lying
Each in his lonely night, each with a ghost.
    Some share that night. But they know, love grows colder,
Grows false and dull, that was sweet lies at most.
    Astonishment is no more in hand or shoulder,
But darkens, and dies out from kiss to kiss.
All this is love; and all love is but this.

Unfortunate

Heart, you are restless as a paper scrap
   That's tossed down dusty pavements by the wind;
   Saying, 'She is most wise, patient and kind.
Between the small hands folded in her lap
Surely a shamed head may bow down at length,
   And find forgiveness where the shadows stir
About her lips, and wisdom in her strength,
   Peace in her peace. Come to her, come to her!' . . .

She will not care. She'll smile to see me come,
   So that I think all Heaven in flower to fold me.
   She'll give me all I ask, kiss me and hold me,
     And open wide upon that holy air
The gates of peace, and take my tiredness home,
     Kinder than God. But, heart, she will not care.

The Chilterns

Your hands, my dear, adorable,
    Your lips of tenderness
– Oh, I've loved you faithfully and well,
    Three years, or a bit less.
    It wasn't a success.

Thank God, that's done! and I'll take the road,
    Quit of my youth and you,
The Roman road to Wendover
    By Tring and Lilley Hoo,
    As a free man may do.

For youth goes over, the joys that fly,
    The tears that follow fast;
And the dirtiest things we do must lie
    Forgotten at the last;
    Even Love goes past.

What's left behind I shall not find,
    The splendour and the pain;
The splash of sun, the shouting wind,
    And the brave sting of rain,
    I may not meet again.

But the years, that take the best away,
    Give something in the end;
And a better friend than love have they,
    For none to mar or mend,
    That have themselves to friend.

I shall desire and I shall find
    The best of my desires;
The autumn road, the mellow wind
    That soothes the darkening shires,
    And laughter, and inn-fires.

White mist about the black hedgerows,
    The slumbering Midland plain,
The silence where the clover grows,
    And the dead leaves in the lane,
    Certainly, these remain.

And I shall find some girl perhaps,
    And a better one than you,
With eyes as wise, but kindlier,
    And lips as soft, but true.
    And I daresay she will do.

Home

I came back late and tired last night
   Into my little room,
To the long chair and the firelight
   And comfortable gloom.

But as I entered softly in
   I saw a woman there,
The line of neck and cheek and chin,
   The darkness of her hair,
The form of one I did not know
   Sitting in my chair.

I stood a moment fierce and still,
   Watching her neck and hair.
I made a step to her; and saw
   That there was no one there.

It was some trick of the firelight
   That made me see her there.
It was a chance of shade and light
   And the cushion in the chair.

Oh, all you happy over the earth,
   That night, how could I sleep?
I lay and watched the lonely gloom;
   And watched the moonlight creep
From wall to basin, round the room.
   All night I could not sleep.

The Night Journey

Hands and lit faces eddy to a line;
  The dazed last minutes click; the clamour dies.
Beyond the great-swung arc o' the roof, divine,
  Night, smoky-scarv'd, with thousand coloured eyes

Glares the imperious mystery of the way.
  Thirsty for dark, you feel the long-limbed train
Throb, stretch, thrill motion, slide, pull out and sway,
  Strain for the far, pause, draw to strength again . . .

As a man, caught by some great hour, will rise,
  Slow-limbed, to meet the light or find his love;
And, breathing long, with staring sightless eyes,
  Hands out, head back, agape and silent, move

Sure as a flood, smooth as a vast wind blowing;
  And, gathering power and purpose as he goes,
Unstumbling, unreluctant, strong, unknowing,
  Borne by a will not his, that lifts, that grows,

Sweep out to darkness, triumphing in his goal,
  Out of the fire, out of the little room . . .
– There is an end appointed, O my soul!
  Crimson and green the signals burn; the gloom

Is hung with steam's far-blowing livid streamers.
  Lost into God, as lights in light, we fly,
Grown one with will, end-drunken huddled dreamers.
  The white lights roar. The sounds of the world die.

And lips and laughter are forgotten things.
   Speed sharpens; grows. Into the night, and on,
The strength and splendour of our purpose swings.
   The lamps fade; and the stars. We are alone.

Song

All suddenly the wind comes soft,
  And Spring is here again;
And the hawthorn quickens with buds of green,
  And my heart with buds of pain.

My heart all Winter lay so numb,
  The earth so dead and frore,
That I never thought the Spring would come,
  Or my heart wake any more.

But Winter's broken and earth has woken,
  And the small birds cry again;
And the hawthorn hedge puts forth its buds,
  And my heart puts forth its pain.

Beauty and Beauty

When Beauty and Beauty meet
   All naked, fair to fair,
The earth is crying-sweet,
   And scattering-bright the air,
Eddying, dizzying, closing round,
   With soft and drunken laughter;
Veiling all that may befall
   After – after –

Where Beauty and Beauty met,
   Earth's still a-tremble there,
And winds are scented yet,
   And memory-soft the air,
Bosoming, folding glints of light,
   And shreds of shadowy laughter;
Not the tears that fill the years
   After – after –

The Way that Lovers use

The way that lovers use is this;
  They bow, catch hands, with never a word,
And their lips meet, and they do kiss,
  – So I have heard.

They queerly find some healing so,
  And strange attainment in the touch;
There is a secret lovers know,
  – I have read as much.

And theirs no longer joy nor smart,
  Changing or ending, night or day;
But mouth to mouth, and heart on heart,
  – So lovers say.

Mary and Gabriel

Young Mary, loitering once her garden way,
Felt a warm splendour grow in the April day,
As wine that blushes water through. And soon,
Out of the gold air of the afternoon,
One knelt before her: hair he had, or fire,
Bound back above his ears with golden wire,
Baring the eager marble of his face.
Not man's nor woman's was the immortal grace
Rounding the limbs beneath that robe of white,
And lighting the proud eyes with changeless light,
Incurious. Calm as his wings, and fair,
That presence filled the garden.

                           She stood there,
Saying, 'What would you, Sir?'

                              He told his word,
'Blessed art thou of women!' Half she heard,
Hands folded and face bowed, half long had known,
The message of that clear and holy tone,
That fluttered hot sweet sobs about her heart;
Such serene tidings moved such human smart.
Her breath came quick as little flakes of snow.
Her hands crept up her breast. She did but know
It was not hers. She felt a trembling stir
Within her body, a will too strong for her
That held and filled and mastered all. With eyes
Closed, and a thousand soft short broken sighs,
She gave submission; fearful, meek, and glad . . .

     She wished to speak. Under her breasts she had
Such multitudinous burnings, to and fro,
And throbs not understood; she did not know
If they were hurt or joy for her; but only
That she was grown strange to herself, half lonely,

All wonderful, filled full of pains to come
And thoughts she dare not think, swift thoughts and dumb,
Human, and quaint, her own, yet very far,
Divine, dear, terrible, familiar . . .
Her heart was faint for telling; to relate
Her limbs' sweet treachery, her strange high estate,
Over and over, whispering, half revealing,
Weeping; and so find kindness to her healing.
'Twixt tears and laughter, panic hurrying her,
She raised her eyes to that fair messenger.
He knelt unmoved, immortal; with his eyes
Gazing beyond her, calm to the calm skies;
Radiant, untroubled in his wisdom, kind.
His sheaf of lilies stirred not in the wind.
How should she, pitiful with mortality,
Try the wide peace of that felicity
With ripples of her perplexed shaken heart,
And hints of human ecstasy, human smart,
And whispers of the lonely weight she bore,
And how her womb within was hers no more
And at length hers?
                    Being tired, she bowed her head;
And said, 'So be it!'
                    The great wings were spread,
Showering glory on the fields, and fire.
The whole air, singing, bore him up, and higher,
Unswerving, unreluctant. Soon he shone
A gold speck in the gold skies; then was gone.

The air was colder, and grey. She stood alone.

The Funeral of Youth: Threnody

The day that *Youth* had died,
There came to his grave-side,
In decent mourning, from the county's ends,
Those scatter'd friends
Who had lived the boon companions of his prime,
And laughed with him and sung with him and wasted,
In feast and wine and many-crown'd carouse,
The days and nights and dawnings of the time
When *Youth* kept open house,
Nor left untasted
Aught of his high emprise and ventures dear,
No quest of his unshar'd –
All these, with loitering feet and sad head bar'd,
Followed their old friend's bier.
Folly went first,
With muffled bells and coxcomb still revers'd;
And after trod the bearers, hat in hand –
Laughter, most hoarse, and Captain *Pride* with tanned
And martial face all grim, and fussy *Joy*,
Who had to catch a train, and *Lust*, poor, snivelling
    boy;
These bore the dear departed.
Behind them, broken-hearted,
Came *Grief*, so noisy a widow, that all said,
'Had he but wed
Her elder sister *Sorrow*, in her stead!'
And by her, trying to soothe her all the time,
The fatherless children, *Colour*, *Tune*, and *Rhyme*
(The sweet lad *Rhyme*), ran all-uncomprehending.
Then, at the way's sad ending,
Round the raw grave they stay'd. Old *Wisdom* read,
In mumbling tone, the Service for the Dead.

There stood *Romance*,
The furrowing tears had mark'd her rougèd cheek;
Poor old *Conceit*, his wonder unassuaged;
Dead *Innocency's* daughter, *Ignorance*;
And shabby, ill-dress'd *Generosity*;
And *Argument*, too full of woe to speak;
Passion, grown portly, something middle-aged;
And *Friendship* – not a minute older, she;
Impatience, ever taking out his watch;
Faith, who was deaf, and had to lean, to catch
Old *Wisdom's* endless drone.
Beauty was there.
Pale in her black; dry-eyed; she stood alone.
Poor maz'd *Imagination*; *Fancy* wild;
Ardour, the sunlight on his greying hair;
Contentment, who had known *Youth* as a child
And never seen him since. And *Spring* came too,
Dancing over the tombs, and brought him flowers –
She did not stay for long.
And *Truth*, and *Grace*, and all the merry crew,
The laughing *Winds* and *Rivers*, and lithe *Hours*;
And *Hope*, the dewy-eyed; and sorrowing *Song* –
Yes, with much woe and mourning general,
At dead *Youth's* funeral,
Even these were met once more together, all,
Who erst the fair and living *Youth* did know;
All, except only *Love*. *Love* had died long ago.

The Old Vicarage, Grantchester
(CAFÉ DES WESTENS, BERLIN, MAY 1912)

Just now the lilac is in bloom,
All before my little room;
And in my flower-beds, I think,
Smile the carnation and the pink;
And down the borders, well I know,
The poppy and the pansy blow . . .
Oh! there the chestnuts, summer through,
Beside the river make for you
A tunnel of green gloom, and sleep
Deeply above; and green and deep
The stream mysterious glides beneath,
Green as a dream and deep as death.
– Oh, damn! I know it! and I know
How the May fields all golden show,
And when the day is young and sweet,
Gild gloriously the bare feet
That run to bathe . . .
                    Du lieber Gott!

Here am I, sweating, sick, and hot,
And there the shadowed waters fresh
Lean up to embrace the naked flesh.
Temperamentvoll German Jews
Drink beer around – and *there* the dews
Are soft beneath a morn of gold.
Here tulips bloom as they are told;
Unkempt about those hedges blows
An English unofficial rose;
And there the unregulated sun
Slopes down to rest when day is done,

And wakes a vague unpunctual star,
A slippered Hesper; and there are
Meads towards Haslingfield and Coton
Where *das Betreten*'s not *verboten*.

εἴθε γενοίμην . . . would I were
In Grantchester, in Grantchester –
Some, it may be, can get in touch
With Nature there, or Earth, or such.
And clever modern men have seen
A Faun a-peeping through the green,
And felt the Classics were not dead,
To glimpse a Naiad's reedy head,
Or hear the Goat-foot piping low: . . .
But these are things I do not know.
I only know that you may lie
Day long and watch the Cambridge sky,
And, flower-lulled in sleepy grass,
Hear the cool lapse of hours pass,
Until the centuries blend and blur
In Grantchester, in Grantchester . . .
Still in the dawnlit waters cool
His ghostly Lordship swims his pool,
And tries the strokes, essays the tricks,
Long learnt on Hellespont, or Styx.
Dan Chaucer hears his river still
Chatter beneath a phantom mill.
Tennyson notes, with studious eye,
How Cambridge waters hurry by . . .
And in that garden, black and white,
Creep whispers through the grass all night;
And spectral dance, before the dawn,
A hundred Vicars down the lawn;
Curates, long dust, will come and go
On lissom, clerical, printless toe;

And oft between the boughs is seen
The sly shade of a Rural Dean . . .
Till, at a shiver in the skies,
Vanishing with Satanic cries,
The prim ecclesiastic rout
Leaves but a startled sleeper-out,
Grey heavens, the first bird's drowsy calls,
The falling house that never falls.

God! I will pack, and take a train,
And get me to England once again!
For England's the one land, I know,
Where men with Splendid Hearts may go;
And Cambridgeshire, of all England,
The shire for Men who Understand;
And of *that* district I prefer
The lovely hamlet Grantchester.
For Cambridge people rarely smile,
Being urban, squat, and packed with guile;
And Royston men in the far South
Are black and fierce and strange of mouth;
At Over they fling oaths at one,
And worse than oaths at Trumpington,
And Ditton girls are mean and dirty,
And there's none in Harston under thirty,
And folks in Shelford and those parts
Have twisted lips and twisted hearts,
And Barton men make Cockney rhymes,
And Coton's full of nameless crimes,
And things are done you'd not believe
At Madingley, on Christmas Eve.
Strong men have run for miles and miles,
When one from Cherry Hinton smiles;
Strong men have blanched, and shot their wives,
Rather than send them to St Ives;

Strong men have cried like babes, bydam,
To hear what happened at Babraham.
But Grantchester! ah, Grantchester!
There's peace and holy quiet there,
Great clouds along pacific skies,
And men and women with straight eyes,
Lithe children lovelier than a dream,
A bosky wood, a slumbrous stream,
And little kindly winds that creep
Round twilight corners, half asleep.
In Grantchester their skins are white;
They bathe by day, they bathe by night;
The women there do all they ought;
The men observe the Rules of Thought.
They love the Good; they worship Truth;
They laugh uproariously in youth;
(And when they get to feeling old,
They up and shoot themselves, I'm told) . . .
　　Ah God! to see the branches stir
Across the moon at Grantchester!
To smell the thrilling-sweet and rotten
Unforgettable, unforgotten
River-smell, and hear the breeze
Sobbing in the little trees.
Say, do the elm-clumps greatly stand
Still guardians of that holy land?
The chestnuts shade, in reverend dream,
The yet unacademic stream?
Is dawn a secret shy and cold
Anadyomene, silver-gold?
And sunset still a golden sea
From Haslingfield to Madingley?
And after, ere the night is born,
Do hares come out about the corn?
Oh, is the water sweet and cool,

Gentle and brown, above the pool?
And laughs the immortal river still
Under the mill, under the mill?
Say, is there Beauty yet to find?
And Certainty? and Quiet kind?
Deep meadows yet, for to forget
The lies, and truths, and pain? . . . oh! yet
Stands the Church clock at ten to three?
And is there honey still for tea?

A NOTE ON THE TEXT

1914 and Other Poems was published by Sidgwick & Jackson, Ltd.,
3 Adam Street, Adelphi, London, in 1915. It was printed at The
Complete Press, West Norwood, London. In the Bertram Rota
Catalogue 287 (1998) the compiler offers a copy of *1914 and Other
Poems*: 'This, the first printing of Brooke's first collection of
poems, was limited to only 500 copies. It was not until the
thirteenth impression (1916) that the book was published with
a printed dust-jacket.' In fact it was Brooke's second collection,
a very slim volume: 64 pages (two quires precisely); a maximum
page depth of 30 lines, the page size being 4.5 × 6 inches,
with generous margins. It was a memorial volume (Brooke, a
Sub-Lieutenant *en route* to the Dardanelles, had died of sunstroke
and septicaemia) but not elegant in presentation.

Edward Marsh, one of Rupert Brooke's numerous close
friends and a devoted patron, assembled the volume after the
poet's death, conceding that Brooke would have published his
own volume 'this spring, but he did not prepare the present
book for publication'. Marsh did the deed, and the book belongs
to the historic moment of its publishing. There were pressing
agendas: first, *pietas*, to honour a dear friend whom he (and
many others) regarded as the great poet of his generation; then
politics, for it was wartime and Brooke was one of the war's
best-known martyrs. *The Times* carried an encomiastic letter
penned by none other than Winston Churchill (another friend
of Marsh's) identifying in Brooke 'a voice' and 'a note': cometh
the hour, cometh the martyr.

Brooke had written poems of devoted patriotism which were
at once suasive and useful. The book opens with Brooke's most
famous – some regard it as notorious – patriotic sequence '1914',
the reason for his immense popularity as for his unpopularity.
Had Brooke lived to assemble this volume, he might not have
foregrounded '1914'. He wrote the five sonnets fitfully during

his early months in the Anson Battalion (Royal Naval Division), into which Churchill had drawn him. After marking the proofs of the sonnets, he wrote to Marsh, 'My muse, panting all autumn under halberd and cuirass, could but falter these syllables through her vizor. God, they're in the rough, these five camp-children – 4 and 5 are good enough, and there are phrases in the rest.' Henry James's response was more ambiguous. Sent the sonnets by Marsh, he reflected: 'The circumstances (so to call the unspeakable matter) that have conduced to them, and that, taken together, seem to make a sort of huge brazen lap for their congruous beauty, have caused me to read them with an emotion that somehow precludes the critical measure.'

Marsh reports in his 'Note' to the 1918 edition of the *Collected Poems* that he had originally intended his memoir to accompany *1914 and Other Poems*, but in the event it was not included (it runs to almost 150 pages): the poems made their own fanfare. Readers and reviewers knew the tragic story already. Had the poems been ballasted with Marsh's hagiographic memoir they might have travelled less far than they did in the event. *1914 and Other Poems* and the 1918 *Collected* sold over 300,000 in the decade following their publication. 'I think *reading* in wartime right enough,' Brooke wrote shortly before his death. 'But writing requires a longer period of serenity, a more certainly undisturbed subconscious. If the S. C.'s turbulent, one's draught from it is opaque. Witness the first three sonnets [of '1914'].' He is right to consider them in some way unfinished.

All the work in *1914 and Other Poems* dates from 1911 or after: none of the earlier (much of it significant, adult) work finds a place; the voice on which Marsh concentrates is not the one that caused mirth and merriment among the poet's friends but a more sententious, rhetorical mode in keeping with the circumstances of the poet's death and the age's immediate demands.

The book Brooke had originally proposed to Marsh was not a slim volume. 'Rupert announced one evening, sitting half-undressed on his bed, that he had conceived a brilliant scheme. He would write a book of poetry, and publish it as a selection from the works of twelve different writers, six men and six women, all with the most convincing pseudonyms.' Then he and Marsh realized the abundant talents they knew and decided, instead, to launch the *Georgian Poetry* anthologies. Had Brooke had his way, he would have outdone Pessoa with twelve heteronyms and at least two sexes to his voice.

Michael Schmidt